Thomas Jefferson

A PICTURE BOOK BIOGRAPHY

Thomas Jefferson

A PICTURE BOOK BIOGRAPHY

This updated edition
includes the story
of Sally Hemings.

by JAMES CROSS GIBLIN

Illustrated by MICHAEL DOOLING

SCHOLASTIC PAPERBACK NONFICTION

AN IMPRINT OF

SCHOLASTIC

NEW YORK TORONTO LONDON AUCKLAND SYDNEY
MEXICO CITY NEW DELHI HONG KONG BUENOS AIRES

ACKNOWLEDGMENTS

The following books and articles were especially helpful in my research:

JEFFERSON by Saul K. Padover. New York: Harcourt, Brace and Company, 1942.

JEFFERSON AND HIS TIME, the six-volume biography by Dumas Malone. Boston: Little, Brown and Company, 1948–1981.

THE LIFE OF THOMAS JEFFERSON by Noble E. Cunningham, Jr. Baton Rouge: Louisiana State University Press, 1987.

MONTICELLO: A GUIDEBOOK by Frederick D. Nichols and James A. Bear. Monticello, Virginia: Thomas Jefferson Memorial Foundation, 1982.

THE PORTABLE THOMAS JEFFERSON, edited by Merrill D. Peterson. New York: Viking Penguin, Inc., 1975.

THOMAS JEFFERSON, AN INTIMATE HISTORY by Fawn M. Brodie. New York: W. W. Norton & Company, Inc., 1974.

THOMAS JEFFERSON, HIS LIFE AND WORDS, edited by Nick Beilenson. White Plains, New York: Peter Pauper Press, Inc., 1986.

Articles in the *New York Times* of November 1 and 8, 1998, and March 3 and December 17, 2001, about the DNA evidence linking Thomas Jefferson with Sally Hemings's son, Eston.

I am also indebted to Patricia R. Crook of the Curry School of Education, the University of Virginia, who helped arrange my visits to Monticello.

ISBN 0-439-81067-1

Library of Congress Cataloging-in-Publication Data available.

12 11 10 9 8 7 6 5 4 3 2 1   8 9 10 11/0

Printed in China   62

First Scholastic paperback printing, January 2006

Designed by Marijka Kostiw

Michael Dooling's artwork is rendered in oil paint on canvas. The floral designs used throughout the book are based on actual French wallpaper designs from the 18th century.

for
PHYLLIS BROOKS
and
NADINE MILES,
two teachers
who showed me how
to find the drama
in human lives
— J.C.G.

for

EDNA McILVEEN
— M.D.

WHEN THOMAS JEFFERSON was an old man, he still remembered that day in 1746. He was just three years old and sitting on a pillow high atop a horse. One of his father's slaves held him tight as they rode toward a sun-speckled wood.

The Jefferson family was on the way from their Virginia farm home, Shadwell, to Tuckahoe farm, fifty miles away. Thomas's father had promised his dying friend, William Randolph, that he would move to Tuckahoe and look after Mr. Randolph's three motherless children. Now he was keeping that promise.

At Tuckahoe, Thomas went to a little schoolhouse in the side yard. The only other students were his three sisters, the two Randolph girls, and the Randolph boy — whose name was Thomas also.

Thomas Jefferson loved to read and write compositions, but he was shy about speaking in front of the class. His voice sank into his throat and he could barely be heard. Sometimes the Randolph boy mimicked him, the girls giggled, and the teacher said, "Speak up, Thomas!"

One day Thomas could take it no longer. He slipped out of the schoolhouse and hid behind a shed. There he knelt and said the Lord's Prayer over and over, hoping the Tuckahoe school would end forever.

When Thomas was nine, the Jeffersons returned to Shadwell, but Thomas did not go with them. Instead he was sent to a boarding school where he studied Latin, Greek, and French.

Thomas came home to Shadwell every summer, and his father taught him how to sit a horse and shoot a gun. On summer evenings the two of them would paddle a canoe along the Rivanna River.

Mr. Jefferson died suddenly when Thomas was just fourteen. Now Thomas had to become the man of the family for his mother, sisters, and little brother.

Knowing how much Thomas loved to read, his father had left him his bookcase and all forty of his books. Thomas especially liked the histories of England and a book about the sun, moon, and stars.

The more he read, the more Thomas knew he wanted to go to college. And so, at seventeen, he set off for the College of William and Mary in Williamsburg, Virginia.

Tall and thin, with soft eyes and a softer voice, Thomas made many friends at college. He danced well, played the violin, and flirted with the girls. But he was too shy to think of romance, let alone marriage.

His first love was study. He rose at dawn and read books or attended classes all day. He was curious about everything. One of his teachers said he never knew anyone to ask as many questions as Thomas Jefferson.

After two years at college, Thomas decided to study law in Williamsburg. One day in 1764 he heard a speaker attack the policies of Great Britain and its king. Britain ruled America then, and wanted to impose new taxes on its colony.

The speech made Thomas think about the future of his country. Should America remain loyal to Great Britain or should it seek its independence?

Back home at Shadwell, Thomas began to practice law. He also began to build a home of his own on land he had inherited from his father. It would stand at the top of a high hill, so he named it Monticello, which means "little mountain" in Italian.

Thomas Jefferson had never studied architecture, but he designed Monticello himself with the help of books from Europe. By the fall of 1770, a one-room redbrick building was finished. Thomas moved into it with his books and fiddle while work continued on the main house.

In 1770, Thomas met a lovely young widow, Martha Wayles Skelton. Martha was the daughter of a lawyer in Williamsburg. She loved music as much as Thomas, and accompanied him on the harpsichord when he played his violin.

This time Thomas was not too shy to declare his love. He proposed to Martha, and they were married at her home on New Year's Day, 1772. Afterward, they set out in a snowstorm for Monticello, a hundred miles away.

By the time they arrived at the foot of the mountain, the snow was two feet deep. They had to leave their carriage and proceed on horseback. At last they reached the little red building on top of the hill. Thomas kindled a fire in the fireplace and welcomed Martha to her new home.

The Jeffersons' first child was born in September 1772. It was a girl and they named her Martha after her mother.

The next year, Mrs. Jefferson's father died and left her 11,000 acres of land and 135 slaves. Among them were light-skinned Betty Hemings and her children, including baby Sally. The Jeffersons sold much of the land but kept the slaves. They came to live at Monticello, where they joined the 52 slaves Thomas had inherited from *his* father.

Besides his family and Monticello, Thomas had another responsibility. He had been elected to represent his county in Virginia's House of Burgesses. This group of men helped the royal governor to run the colony. And trouble was brewing with the mother country, Great Britain.

Up north in Boston, rebels protesting a British tax dumped a cargo of tea into the harbor in December 1773. This event became known as the Boston Tea Party. The Virginia House of Burgesses supported the action of their fellow Americans in Massachusetts. They proposed that delegates from all thirteen colonies meet each year in a congress. At the congress they could discuss their common problems.

In the spring of 1776, Thomas attended the Second Continental Congress in Philadelphia. Although he rarely spoke out, everyone knew that Thomas was one of the best writers at the Congress. That is why he was invited to draft America's Declaration of Independence from Great Britain.

It took Thomas seventeen days to write and rewrite the Declaration. He wanted to make sure that every sentence was exactly right. After he gave his finished draft to Congress, the members spent three more days going over it line by line. They changed a word here and cut a phrase there while Thomas suffered silently.

At last, on July 4, 1776, Congress adopted the Declaration of Independence. "We hold these truths to be self-evident, that all men are created equal," it said.

The Declaration listed the crimes of the British king and explained why Americans should fight for their freedom. It was one of the most important documents ever written in the United States.

Back home in Virginia, Thomas urged that the new state enact four groundbreaking laws. One would guarantee religious freedom to everyone in Virginia.

Thomas also favored the end of the slave trade. Hadn't he written that "all men are created equal"? And didn't he believe that slavery was wrong? Yes, but he also knew that estates like his beloved Monticello could not be run without slave labor.

Thomas went back and forth, back and forth about slavery. What should be done about it? He could not make up his mind.

In the North, George Washington was leading the American army in battles against the British. All seemed peaceful in Virginia, however. Thomas was elected governor of the state in 1779. But then, a year later, a large British force landed near the capital, Richmond.

The British tried to capture Thomas at Monticello, but he escaped just in time. Soon afterward the British were defeated at Yorktown. Peace returned to Virginia.

Thomas decided to retire from public life when his term as governor was up. Back at Monticello, he enjoyed his farm, his family, his books and music. But his happiness did not last long.

Over the years, he and his wife had had five children, only two of whom lived. Now, after giving birth to another child in 1782, Mrs. Jefferson herself sickened and died.

Thomas was paralyzed by grief. For three weeks he never left his room. When he came out at last, he asked that his horse be saddled. He rode five miles through the woods that day and every day thereafter. His oldest daughter, Martha, rode with him. She often saw Thomas burst into tears when he thought of her mother.

Jefferson grieved for six months before he became interested in life again. Then, in 1784, he accepted an assignment from Congress. He sailed to France, where he would be a special ambassador in Paris.

Thomas took his daughter Martha with him and left her two sisters with relatives. In Paris, Martha entered a convent school where the teachers were nuns. Thomas presented himself at the court of King Louis XVI.

Word came from America that Thomas's youngest daughter, Lucy, had died of whooping cough.

Once more Jefferson was overcome with sorrow. He arranged for his middle daughter, Polly, to join him and her older sister in France. A fourteen-year-old slave from Monticello, Sally Hemings, made the long journey with Polly.

Through friends, Thomas met several English artists who were visiting Paris. One of them was the beautiful Maria Cosway, who painted miniature portraits. Thomas offered to show Maria the countryside around Paris. They toured ancient castles and ate in inns along the river Seine.

Some say the two of them fell in love. But Thomas had promised his dying wife he would never marry again, and he remembered his vow. He and Maria parted, sadly.

Soon afterward, France exploded into revolution and Thomas was called home to America. President George Washington had a new assignment for him.

Washington wanted Jefferson to be his secretary of state. But first Thomas had to tend to Monticello. While he was in France, the estate had become rundown.

He also had to plan the wedding of his daughter Martha. Just seventeen, she married Thomas Mann Randolph, the son of Jefferson's boyhood friend.

After serving as secretary of state, Jefferson became the vice president under John Adams. And then, in 1801, he was elected president himself.

On inauguration day, Thomas got up early and dressed in a gray waistcoat and green breeches. He left his boardinghouse in the new capital city, Washington, and walked two blocks to the unfinished Capitol.

There he took his oath of office and gave a thoughtful, well-written speech. But only those sitting in the first four rows heard his words. Thomas was still shy about speaking in public.

After his inauguration, Thomas moved into the White House, which was just a year old and was known as the President's House. He lived by himself because his daughters had to stay with their families in Virginia.

At the President's House, Thomas did away with formal gatherings and entertained at small private dinners. The table was round so that no guest would sit in a more important place than another.

A mockingbird kept Thomas company in his study. He loved to listen to its cheerful songs while he worked. If he had no visitors, he let the bird out of its cage so that it could fly freely around the room. Often it would land on his shoulder and chirp in his ear.

As president, Thomas strove for economy at home and peace abroad. His policies were tested when the French leader Napoleon acquired the Louisiana Territory from Spain. Many people feared Napoleon would close the Mississippi River to American ships. Some thought the United States would have to go to war with France to keep the river open.

A war was the last thing Jefferson wanted. Instead, he offered to buy the port city of New Orleans from the French for two million dollars. To his surprise, the French offered to sell him the entire Louisiana Territory for fifteen million dollars!

Thomas was delighted. The Louisiana Territory stretched all the way from the Mississippi to the Rocky Mountains, and contained almost a million square miles. By purchasing it, Thomas doubled the size of the United States. It was one of his greatest accomplishments as president.

However, some people did not benefit from the Louisiana Purchase. Those were the Native Americans who lived in the territory. They had been there for more than a thousand years, but neither France nor the United States honored their claims to the land.

In 1804, Thomas ran for a second term as president and won in a landslide. But a cloud of sadness darkened his triumph. The spring before, his younger daughter, Polly, had died in Virginia at the age of twenty-five. Now, of his six children, only Martha was still alive.

When his second term ended in 1809, Thomas returned to Monticello. There he rose at dawn and read and wrote until breakfast at nine. His house slave, Sally Hemings, made sure his private rooms were always clean and neat.

After breakfast, Thomas mounted his favorite horse, Eagle, and inspected the fields and orchards where his other slaves were at work.

Dinner at Monticello was at three. After it, Thomas read some more and wrote letters to his many friends. He was usually in bed by ten.

His daughter Martha and her family came to live with Thomas. He loved to play with his eleven grandchildren and watch them run races on the lawn. But they knew better than to enter his study without permission. For Thomas, at the age of seventy-five, had begun work on a new project.

Thomas had always believed in the importance of education. If you weren't educated, how could you be a good citizen of a democracy like the United States?

Now he planned a new three-part school system for Virginia. There would be free public elementary schools for all children. Free high schools within one day's ride of every teenager. And a state university in Charlottesville, near Monticello.

The state approved the plan for the university, and for the next six years Thomas devoted himself to it. He designed the main buildings. He hired skilled workmen. And every day the white-haired old man rode down the mountain to Charlottesville to see how construction was going.

At last, in 1825, the University of Virginia was finished and ready to welcome its first students. A proud Thomas Jefferson attended the opening ceremonies. But he was worried, too.

Through the years, Thomas's income had never been enough to cover his expenses. He had gone deeper and deeper into debt. And now he was in danger of losing Monticello.

To raise money, Thomas had sold one of the things he loved most — his library. The U.S. Congress bought the six thousand books in it for $25,000. The books were added to the nation's library, the Library of Congress in Washington.

The money from Congress helped, but Thomas's debts had continued to mount. Now he feared he would have to sell every piece of property he owned to pay his creditors. And then he would have nothing to leave his family.

News of his troubles spread, and people all across the country were shocked. How could such a thing be happening to Thomas Jefferson? Committees in New York, Philadelphia, Baltimore, and other cities raised thousands of dollars for Thomas. Smaller gifts came from farms and villages in both North and South, and outposts on the Western frontier.

Thomas was overwhelmed by this offering of love. Thanks to the generosity of the American people, Monticello had been saved for the moment. Now the eighty-three-year-old Thomas could make his will and prepare to die in his beloved home.

To each of his grandchildren, Thomas left a gold watch. The girls would receive theirs when they turned sixteen, the boys when they were twenty-one.

Unlike George Washington, Thomas did not make plans to free his slaves after his death. He had always been opposed to the *idea* of slavery. At the same time, he had always depended on slaves to keep Monticello going — and he still did. In his will, he freed only five male slaves, all of them members of Sally Hemings' family. Sally herself was not freed until later, by Thomas's daughter Martha.

By the end of June 1826, Thomas knew he was dying. But he was determined to live until July 4th. It would be the fiftieth anniversary of the signing of the Declaration of Independence, and he wanted to see that day.

At night on the third, Thomas asked his doctor, "Is it the Fourth?" "It soon will be," the doctor said, and Thomas smiled. The next day, a little past noon on the Fourth, he died.

Before his death, Thomas had written the words he wanted to have inscribed on his tomb at Monticello. They said nothing about the Louisiana Purchase or his other accomplishments as president. Instead, they listed the following things he hoped he would be remembered for:

AUTHOR OF THE
DECLARATION OF AMERICAN INDEPENDENCE
OF THE
STATUTE OF VIRGINIA FOR RELIGIOUS FREEDOM
AND FATHER OF THE UNIVERSITY OF VIRGINIA

IMPORTANT DATES IN THOMAS JEFFERSON'S LIFE

April 2, 1743 — Thomas Jefferson is born at Shadwell farm in what is now Albemarle County, Virginia. (In 1752, the calendar was changed and Thomas's birthday now falls on April 13.)

August 17, 1757 — Thomas's father, Peter Jefferson, dies at Shadwell.

March 25, 1760 — Thomas enters the College of William and Mary in Williamsburg, Virginia.

February 1767 — Thomas begins to practice law in Albemarle County.

1769 — Thomas begins to build Monticello.

January 1, 1772 — Thomas marries Martha Wayles Skelton.

1775–1776 — Jefferson serves as a member of the Continental Congress.

June 11–June 28, 1776 — Jefferson writes the Declaration of Independence.

July 4, 1776 — Congress adopts the Declaration of Independence.

1779–1781 — Jefferson serves as Governor of Virginia.

September 6, 1782 — Thomas's wife Martha dies.

1784–1789 — Thomas lives in Paris where he is an ambassador to France.

1790–1793 — Jefferson serves as U.S. secretary of state.

1797–1801 — Jefferson is vice president of the United States.

February 17, 1801 — Jefferson is elected to his first term as president.

May 2, 1803 — The United States purchases the Louisiana Territory from France.

1804 — Jefferson is reelected president.

1809 — Jefferson completes his second term and retires to Monticello.

March 7, 1825 — The University of Virginia opens.

July 4, 1826 — Thomas Jefferson dies at Monticello.

THE WORDS OF THOMAS JEFFERSON

From youth to old age, Thomas Jefferson never stopped writing. Not just the Declaration of Independence and other public statements and speeches, but books, essays, and thousands of letters to friends. Here are a few of the thoughts and ideas that he expressed in his letters:

⚜

"This ball of liberty, I believe most piously, is now so well in motion that it will roll round the globe." (From a 1795 letter to Tench Coxe)

⚜⚜

"Were it left for me to decide whether we should have a government without newspapers or newspapers without a government, I should not hesitate a moment to prefer the latter. But I should mean that every man . . . be capable of reading them." (From a 1787 letter to Edward Carrington)

⚜⚜⚜

"I place economy among the first and most important of republican virtues, and public debt as the greatest of the dangers to be feared." (From an 1816 letter to William Plumer)

⚜⚜

"I have ever thought religion a concern purely between our God and our consciences . . . I never told my own religion nor scrutinized that of another. I never attempted to make a convert nor wished to change another's creed." (From an 1816 letter to Mrs. Samuel H. Smith)

⚜

"I thank you sincerely for your letter of the 19th instant and for the Almanac it contained. No body wishes more than I do to see such proofs as you exhibit, that nature has given to our black brethren talents equal to those of the other colors of men, and that the appearance of a want of them is owing merely to the degraded conditions of their existence, both in Africa and America." (From a 1791 letter to the free-born black scientist Benjamin Banneker)

✦✦✦

"He who permits himself to tell a lie once, finds it much easier to do it a second and a third time, till at length it becomes habitual; he tells lies without attending to it, and truths without the world's believing him."
(From a 1785 letter to Peter Carr)

✦✦

"With respect to the distribution of your time the following is what I should approve.

    from 8. to 10 o'clock practice music
    from 10. to 1. dance one day and draw another
    from 1. to 2. draw on the day you dance,
            and write a letter the next day
    from 3. to 4. read French
    from 4. to 5. exercise yourself in music
    from 5. till bedtime read English, write etc.

I expect you will write to me by every post. Inform me what books you read, what tunes you learn, and inclose me your best copy of every lesson in drawing.... Take care that you never spell a word wrong. Always before you write a word consider how it is spelt, and if you do not remember it, turn to a dictionary. It produces great praise to a lady to spell well." (From a 1783 letter to his daughter, Martha, age eleven)

"Be a listener only, keep within yourself, and endeavor to establish with yourself the habit of silence, especially in politics." (From an 1808 letter to his grandson, Thomas Jefferson Randolph)

✦✦

"I have often thought that nothing would do more extensive good at small expense than the establishment of a small circulating library in every county...." (From an 1809 letter to John Wyche)

✦✦✦

"All my wishes end where I hope my days will end ... at Monticello." (From an 1820 letter to Maria Cosway)

SALLY HEMINGS'S STORY

Over the years, there have been many rumors about Sally Hemings. After Thomas Jefferson's wife died, some people said that the young house slave at Monticello was closer to Jefferson than anyone else. They even claimed that Jefferson was the father of Sally's children.

Most historians dismissed their claims, arguing that there was no evidence whatsoever that Jefferson maintained a secret family. But then in 1998, scientists made a startling discovery. They performed DNA tests on blood samples taken from a living male descendant of the Jefferson line, and from a direct descendant of Sally Hemings's youngest son, Eston. They found that the Y-chromosomes in the two samples matched perfectly. Now there was clear scientific evidence that Thomas Jefferson was the father of at least one of Sally Hemings's children.

The discovery forced people to rethink their views of Jefferson. "It reminds us of a truth that should be self-evident," wrote historian Joseph Ellis. "Our heroes — and especially our presidents — are not gods or saints, but flesh-and-blood humans."

It raised new questions about Sally Hemings, too. Who was she exactly, and what was her relationship to Thomas Jefferson?

Sally was the daughter of Betty Hemings, a slave in the household of John Wayles, Thomas Jefferson's father-in-law. After Mr. Wayles's wife died, he became involved with Betty Hemings. Sally Hemings was born some time later, and everyone on the Wayles plantation assumed that John Wayles was the baby's father. If this was true, Sally was the half-sister of Martha Wayles Jefferson, Thomas's wife.

Such things happened often in the days of slavery. A master owned his slaves, so he thought he could do whatever he wanted with them. The slaves risked punishment or even death if they resisted.

After Thomas Wayles himself died in 1773, little Sally and her mother came to Monticello to live. They were part of Mrs. Jefferson's inheritance from her father. Nothing is recorded of Sally's childhood at Monticello, but she must have stood out among the other young slaves. For, in 1787, after Mrs. Jefferson's death, she was chosen to accompany Jefferson's younger daughter, Polly, to Paris.

Sally was then fourteen. A fellow slave described her as "very handsome, and mighty near white, with long straight hair down her back." She may have looked very much like her half-sister, Thomas Jefferson's late wife.

Sally stayed in Paris with Jefferson and his daughters for over two years. Shortly after her return to Monticello, she gave birth to her first child, Tom. As the boy grew up, many visitors to Monticello commented on his resemblance to Thomas Jefferson.

Sally had four more children in the years that followed — three boys, Beverly, Madison, and Eston, and a girl, Harriet. When they were grown, Tom, Beverly, and Harriet all ran away from Monticello. They went to the North, where they lived as whites.

In his will, Thomas Jefferson freed Sally's two younger sons, Madison and Eston. After Jefferson's death, they moved into a small rented house near Monticello. Two years later, Sally herself was freed by Jefferson's daughter, Martha. She joined her sons in their house, and there she died in 1835, at the age of sixty-two.

Thomas Jefferson never mentioned Sally or her children in any of the thousands of letters he wrote. Nor did he speak of her to any of his friends. But he and Sally must have had a close and enduring bond. Jefferson fathered her son Eston in 1808, more than twenty years after Sally joined him in Paris.

After his mother's death, Eston Hemings moved to Madison, Wisconsin, and changed his name to E. H. Jefferson. People who knew Eston said his fair skin made it easy for him to enter white society, and all of his descendants identified themselves as white.

Eston's great-great-grandson John provided the blood sample that proved Thomas Jefferson was Eston's father. When the test results were announced, John Jefferson declined to talk to reporters. But his sister, Julia, was happy to give interviews. "It's such an American thing to have a drop of this [kind of blood] and a drop of that," she said. "I'm Scotch, Irish, English, French, Welsh, and now black."

Not everyone was glad to know that Thomas Jefferson had apparently had a second family with a young slave woman. When the Monticello Association, an organization of Jefferson descendants, met in 1999, some members refused to acknowledge their black relatives.

But John Jefferson's sister, Julia, remained hopeful. "Our family is like a sample family that was deeply divided and then came together," she said. "So think of what an example we can set for America."

INDEX

Page numbers in italic indicate illustrations.